Poetry
Plain & Simple

Celia P. Ransom

Grey Wolfe Publishing, LLC
PO Box 1088
Birmingham, Michigan 48009
www.GreyWolfePublishing.com

© 2014 Grey Wolfe Publishing
Published by Grey Wolfe Publishing, LLC
www.GreyWolfePublishing.com
All Rights Reserved

ISBN: 978-1-62828-037-1
Library of Congress Control Number: 2014947919

Poetry

Plain and Simple

Jerry,
I hope you enjoy
these plain and simple
words! Best wishes,
Celia

Celia P. Ransom

Dedication

To George Preston, my grandfather, a man ahead of his time, who was a great storyteller.

To Jack, my husband, who is my best friend and cheering section.

To my daughter Suzanne and her family who are my inspiration.

To Ellen, my dear friend, who is always there for me, my touchstone.

To my Michigan State University friends who have been bombarded with my poems since this phase in my life began.

Contents

Friendship Plain and Simple

Health Plain and Simple

Loss Plain and Simple

Love Plain and Simple

Memories Plain and Simple

Patriotism Plain and Simple

Thoughts Plain and Simple

Epilogue Plain and Simple

Celia P. Ransom

Friendship

Plain and Simple

A BELOVED FRIEND

How do you say a final goodbye
To a friend from forever about to die?
Do you hold her hand in yours
And thereby hope to extend life's force?
Or do you let her slip from that bond of pain
Even though selfishly you want her to remain?
And without her presence will life ever be the same?
I think not—for when she hears God call her name
You'll have to let her go.

September 2, 2011
For my dear friend Iva Carroll

COOKS

I have friends who are gourmet cooks.
They pour their way through tome-like cookbooks.
And they are always in despair
That I'm not deeply interested in their culinary fare.
A gastronome I certainly am not.
I could care less about what's boilin' in the pot.
'cause I'm one of those who, when hungry, I eat.
Give me an apple and I'm quite complete.
In the kitchen I do not want to stay
For I have much to do in my hectic day.
But to these dear friends who so love fancy soups and
soufflés,
It's okay for you to hang with Julia, I love you
Anyways.

CUP OF TEA

Today I had a cup of tea.
My lost friend's face flashed in front of me.
Tea was what we always shared
'cause for coffee she never cared.
There I sat with hands on cup
Remembering subjects we might have brought up.
Mostly t'would be the foibles of family
But perhaps the world's state, its lack of morality.
Or—at this time of year
It might be the holidays, Christmas being near.
And there I sat without her at my side
The sting of loss, almost more than I could abide.
Looking into my empty cup
Remembering a life to God given up.

FRIENDSHIP

Faces unlined, as teens we met.
Friendship then was permanently set.
O'er the years we've remained connected,
By shared experience guarded, reflected.
Between us we honor this special treasure,
A myriad of memories we cannot measure.

GIRLFRIEND

Girlfriend, girlfriend
What would I do without you?
You listen to me whine, listen to me spew,
You tolerate my tears, I've had a few.
You share your wisdom when I need a boost,
Lend ear to my prattle 'til the chickens roost.
You give me courage when I falter and sway.
You go along with me when I need to play.
You make me laugh, you make me smile,
Time spent with you, so incredibly worthwhile.
So my dear friend, you have my devotion,
For me this friendship is a magic potion.

GIVE HER GRACE

Give her grace.
Have you been in her place?
Have you struggled like she to overcome
The worry of what her children will become?
Should she not be allowed to continue?
To find the appropriate venue
For her family's well being
Without your judging, without you're not seeing
Her difficulty in navigating the harsh economic icon
That daily drags her down.
Be still, give her grace.

LADIES OF THE LUNCH

Ladies of the lunch,
A twosome, threesome or a bunch.
Chitter, chatter is the tune,
'midst clatter of knife, fork or spoon.
The gatherings always are at their pleasure,
But the friendships are the greatest treasure,
For they know well that the bond they share,
Is theirs alone and exceedingly rare.

MARY LOU

A lonely child was I,
And then you came by.
Young, I do not recall exactly how we met,
But after all this time there is caring yet.
Time, space, and experience have separated us,
But you have remained my friend and that's a plus.
In girlhood you brightened for me many sorry days,
For that gift, I shall always sing your praise.

MY CANINE FRIEND

She cocked her head and looked at me
With intelligent eyes, this magnificent Welsh Corgi.
She knew, I swear, that I was sad
For that day lay dead, my dad.
My heart was breaking o'er such tremendous loss
But she settled next to me and with her paws
Touched my arm in a comforting gesture
A simple canine moment that helped lift the pain, the
pressure.
And as I stroked her coat again and again
She was what I needed—a quiet but sympathetic friend.

MY FRIEND

He is my companion, my friend
Our hearts blend.
We are both our own person
But in this love we find immersion.
He is my soul.

PALADIN

Dark thunderous thoughts in my mind sounded.
But you, oh knight, raised my spirits,
Kept me calm, kept me grounded.
You slew the dragons when they abounded.
Stay nigh, oh paladin, stay nigh.

TO DR. CAPONE

It is said that the eyes are the window to the soul
And if this truth be told
When you look into this man's eyes to check
Can you see his kindness there--just a speck?

For this is a man who is loved by many
Never has he done ill to others, not any
He has always endeavored to do his best
In difficult times, even ill and hard pressed.

So should you come to pray
On whatever may be your religious day
Would you tell your God just for me
Of the goodness in his eyes that I hope you see.

TO HOWARD

Two loaves of bread was what I needed
Seeing you, that was what I repeated.
And thus through no pre-conceived plan
Our special acquaintance that day began.

Though we do not meet each week,
When we do we always speak
Sharing a laugh and a smile
As we chat, if but for a little while.

In age we are years apart
But a connection was there from the start.
And as we discuss the human condition
Each of us offers his own rendition

Oft we find that we are in accord
Our exchanges being their own reward.
When with a fond goodbye we conclude
I'm always warmed by such a pleasant interlude.

SPECIAL FRIEND

Her presence warms me with her sense of fun,
For she is my friend, the very one
Who lifts my spirit with her good intention
When my troubles overwhelm at the very mention.

Soon because of her listening and rapt concern
My life seems less dour and laughter does return.
In need, I prevail on her magic so warm hearted
And carry it with me once departed.

Health

Plain and Simple

ASSAULT

I clasped your hand in mine
Assured you that all would be fine
You looked into my eyes
And knew with those few words I had lied.

For with one more procedure they would claim
More of your body, another assault all the same.
And your life would never again be whole,
Nor ours together, truth be told.

DEMENTIA'S DEMONS

The demons are rising
Tearing at memory
Erasing cognition, all logical thought
Causing confusion more often than not
Stories repeated
Ideas not completed
A look askance
Or a vacant glance.
Family and friends, strangers all
As the insidious disease casts its pall.

EMERGENCY ROOM

Once again behind a privacy curtain.
For my guy 'tis not a good thing, that's for certain.
Twenty times we repeat the reason for our arrival.
Basic, of course, it's just survival.

Poking and prodding by scrub wearing minions,
Offering us separate and oft differing opinions.
And here we are patient and mate,
Helpless, dependent on others to decide our fate.

Too young these physicians look to know any truth,
Or am I just too suspicious of today's youth?
Faith I must have that they're up to the task,
As they practice their art, gloved and masked.

GERIATRIC

Geriatric, does that term apply to me?
I did not think that it could ever be.
But of late, with no more color in my hair,
I think I have to give up and declare
That possibly others' perception of me,
Includes thoughts of frailty and/or senility.
And with my current white headed block.
I hear "sweetie" and "dearie"; an answer that is stock.
Oh, woe, I've passed the stage that used to be "ma'am"
And suddenly I no longer recognize who I am.

IT'S TIME

When your body deserts you,
But your brain is quite fine
Perhaps then you'll know that it is time
To draw in sand a definitive line
And inform your esteemed medical collection
You no longer desire their pharmaceutical selection
Except for that one last contribution from Morpheus.
Eternal rest.

KILLING ME

Is something killing me?
An insidious disease I cannot perceive?
I'm always concerned when I see
Physicians presenting dire messages on TV.
Should it be my time to confront an ill head on,
Will I be brave, will I be calm?
And should I lose the fight, go down to defeat
With no reason left for my life to compete
Will I be able to fearlessly and gracefully slip away?

LET ME GO

Oh, Lord,
Leave me be!
Let my soul rest!
There's no more of me to give.
Not much time to live.
I need to find peace,
To be ready for release.
Please just can't you agree?
Leave me be!
Let me go!

MY BODY

It is ever so difficult to explain
My body just isn't in keeping with my brain.
Run, run says the mind, feel the wind in your face
But, alas, the legs can barely get up to pace.
What happened to those carefree skipping days?
How cruel the brain, the tricks it plays.
Active, I see myself ever so vividly
But my body just reacts with perfidy.

WAITING

Waiting with others all in a room.
Wondering about status, joy or doom
Of a loved one beleaguered with an ill
Hoping against hope he'll survive by sheer will.
But what if...

Loss

Plain and Simple

ABED

I lie in my bed,
Pondering the day ahead.
Knowing that when I arise,
The day before me will contain no prize,
But much of the same,
Filled with sadness and pain.
So a while longer I'll stay in place,
Gathering courage for what I must face.

ALL ALONE

She was alone.
The end came at night.
I know not if she tried to fight
To hold on to her feeble existence
Or if there was any resistance.
She was all alone!
I was not there!

CANCELED

Dreams busted
As though splattered on a hot steamy pavement.
Plans harshly negated.
All lost
Canceled by insidious weakening disease.
I cry silently.

CHANGE

I'm making my adieu.
I'm done, I'm through.
I can no longer look you in the face.
I can't keep up the pace.
You have sabotaged me for the last time.
I'll be moving on to a healthier clime.
Help is what you need but deny.
This reason for my overdue goodbye.
I held on as long as I could
Hoping that in time you would...
Change.

COFFINS

Twenty little ones in coffins laid
Along with teachers who tried valiantly those lives to save.
In time, this horrific memory will fade
Until we learn of more lethal bullets sprayed.
Then the reminder will be there poignantly once more
Of the terror, savagery and the bravery of before.

CRACKED

Something inside me cracked.
Perhaps it was my heart.
'cause he left, gone forever more.
Even tho' with words and kisses, I did implore
That he stay with me.
He didn't have to go, it didn't have to be.
And now here I am in pain.
He's gone.
He left
And something inside me cracked!

DISAPPOINTMENT

My dreams were puffed up. They allowed me to soar.
Imagination said falsely, "there would be more".
But life never played out the way it should be,
I was always in the wings, waiting, you see.
When reality struck, ever so hard,
It cracked me and broke me like a pottery shard.
Struggling with disappointment, heavy with loss,
I just gave up! I dropped the cross!

DRIED UP

I've dried up, no thinking
I watch gore around me without blinking
Emotionally I cannot comprehend
The evil that man perpetrates without end.
Where is the compassion for our fellow man?
What drives such hatred, is it a plan
To tear the world completely asunder?
I know not, I can only wonder.
I've dried up!

DYING

She laughed and smiled,
But she knew he was dying.
She chatted and lunched with friends,
But she knew he was dying.
She shopped weekly, routinely,
But she knew he was dying.
She read the paper, paid the bills,
But she knew he was dying.
She telephoned family, solved problems,
But she knew he was dying.
She celebrated birthdays for young and old,
But she knew he was dying.
She sat alone crying,
Because she knew he was dying.
Would life be the same,
When no longer anyone said his name?

ENNUI

I look at life with a jaundiced eye,
Watching the days, months, years go by.
For me what is there up ahead?
Why even bother to rise from bed?
To face the constant ennui,
That consumes and overwhelms me?

FINAL CONVERSATION

What did your mother tell you when dying?
Did she advise you, when down, to keep on trying?
Did she say, be good to your brother
Because he is your only, there is no other?
Did she remind you to be attentive to your wife
For she is the one who gave your children life?
Did she tell you to take care, slow down,
To revel in the blessings you have all around?
Did she share experiences from her life's span
Hoping to encourage you, her boy, now a man?
Did she tell you how much she cared
For you, her son and the love you both shared?
Did she heap praise on what a good son you'd been?
And were you there to hold her hand at the end?

FOREVER LOST

I think I have lost you forever.
You used to be mine, my treasure.
But you have taken a path unfamiliar to me.
I am disappointed in what you have come to be.
I no longer know who you are.
How could you have gone so far...
Away.

GRIEF

Grief comes in a flicker or a wave.
You never quite know how to behave.
What can you do with left over love, set apart
That still remains locked in your saddened heart?
Each day is much the same
A singular moment while dealing with the pain
Of love and loss...

INDISCRETION

Whispers of indiscretion
How shameful, painful
Questions afloat
O'er an emotionally open moat
Of aspersions cast
Ugly mention long last
Lives ne'er to be the same
Love lost, no trust can remain.

KNOCKIN'

I knocked at your door.
I'd been there many times before.
But you were gone, not there anymore.
You had said you were leavin'
But my head and heart just weren't believin'
That you would truly go without a goodbye
'cause ready I was for another try.
But you, my love, were not into stayin' around
Maybe you already had someone new in a neighborin' town
I should've come by sooner, not let pride get in the way
Then perhaps I could've convinced you not to go, just stay.

LEAVIN'

I told you I was leavin' t'would just be awhile
But the wheels kept a'rollin' mile after mile.
I still see your face, tears streamin' down
Hauntin' my mind as I travel town to town.
Will you still be there waitin' when I return
Or will that yellow ribbon be black is my constant
concern?
Yes, I told you I was leavin' t'would just be awhile
But the wheels keep a movin' mile after mile.

LET HER GO

I may have to let her go,
Because I am losing me.
My reflection in her eyes,
Is not what it used to be.
I do not want to end up singing that sad song,
When finally she says that to me she doesn't want to
belong.
I have to let her go
I'll be so lost, I know.

LIVING TOO LONG

Lonely and alone
Hearing the wind, its mournful moan.
No one with whom to share.
By myself, no one single soul to care
Whether I'm happy or full of dread
Whether I'm alive or dead.
This is the way I perceive the future to be
'cause now everyone I've loved is gone, you see.

LOOKIN'

When it's over, it's over.
What more to say?
There was nothin' I could do to make him stay
For he had eyes for another he thought better
A fancy woman, a real high stepper.

Nothin's left of that love he had for me
So I just have to let it go, let it be.
But not much worry about me, sister
'cause I'll be a lookin' for a brand new mister.

LOST LOVE

It was a love that could have been.
Feelings were there and might be again,
If just one of us took the first step,
To cross the bridge to a love we left.

MASSACRE

Reports circulating of another massacre
With no answers as to why these events occur.
A randomness so unexpected, so unpredictable.
No evidence abounds that these acts are cyclical.
There seem to be enraged shooters in legion
Attacks instigated in no defined region.
Domestic terrorism is the given name
Assigned to this bloodbath, this horrific end game.
Often the crazed perpetrator commits suicide.
A defiant statement in his mind to make his act bona fide.
Leaving the many, stunned, wounded, dead and grieving.
Knowing no answers for them will be there worth
believing.
With so many innocents maimed and lost
Can those affected find solace and at what cost?

MORTALITY

Of late far too often I hear the word mortality
But never have I in reality
Thought of owning it as mine,
For I am always feeling hale, feeling fine.
But all about me there is decided change
Those I love are suffering, some in intense pain
And others in my life have already passed.
Should mortality be part of my vocabulary at last?

NO MORE

When I see you no more.
When from my eyes tears pour.
How will I be able to continue,
When I'll no longer be with you?
What will a solitary life bring?
Just winter, no hint of spring.

ON THE LOSS OF A FRIEND

Oh, how it hurts when we lose a friend,
One who with us spent time on end,
With whom we've shared both laughter and pain
We ask, "Will it ever be the same?"
The answer, I give, is—"I think not."
But their essence and memories will ne'er be forgot.
And in time when we recall
Those best times of all,
We'll smile as we remember.

PAIN

She was the thread that connected me
To a past life encumbered, not free.
And yet, she told me little
To give me hope as I pushed through the middle
Of torments and secrets, so many untold
Which revealed would have sent me into life's fray far
more bold.
She seemed to lack courage to disclaim
What would have comforted me, perhaps assuaged
(eased) my pain.

SHOOTINGS

Lives lost today in senseless tragedy.
Young ones and older ones at their zenith.
Dreams eternally shattered in an horrific instant of terror.
Families and friends left in abject despair
Asking God in his wisdom, how is this fair?
Why more and more does this dark social drama play?
Can't there be better solution, isn't there a way
To calm troubled souls feeling so bereft
Whose only way to absolution is to select a pathway of
death?

SPIRIT

I am left with but a glimmering of spirit.
The joyful voice of youth, no longer do I hear it.
My days are filled with infirmity and weakness.
My vision perpetually clouded with bleakness.
Those voices that speak of triumph of spirit, I find
Fall hollow on my encumbered mind.
Always I have tried to follow the positive path
But now am beaten down by life's circumstance
With its resounding wrath.
This surely must be the darkened end.
My heart is broken, my spirit will not mend.

SOFTLY

She said his name softly.
There was a tenderness in her eyes.
I knew then there was to be a change in our lives.
That soon I'd be just another
Cast aside lover,
Losing my place as significant other.

What could I do about her selection?
Should I fight, claw my way back to her affection?
Or just be still, leaving hurtful words unspoken
Gracefully retreating, though heartbroken?
And thus as a man cling tightly to my pride,
Resenting all the while the other at her side?

THE MAN ON THE GRATE

I saw him, homeless, resting on a steamy grate.
What brought him there, was it just fate?
I gave him all the money that I had,
Not nearly enough, for his situation was bad.
Wrapped he was in a blanket tattered and worn,
Shoes with soles ripped and torn.
No impediment against terrific cold,
In a terrible environment uncontrolled.

That image did not leave my mind
And the next day I went to find
A warm coat, hat, and boots fleece lined.
I found him there in that same iron place
Steamy vapors surrounding his face.
Cocooned he was in his remnant,
Face etched, body spent.
And although something he had not sought
To him I presented the clothing I had brought
And as I shook him to awake
I realized sadly, I was too late.

THE PAST

Why didn't I ask?
When near
And they were here
About their past.
Where they came from
Their dreams when young
Why didn't I ask?

Now they're gone.
I am here.
No one asks
About my past.
Where I came from.
What dreams were mine.
Why don't they ask?

THE SHOOTER

The solitary mass shooter—is he concerned about dying
alone?
And for that reason he can condone
The shooting down of defenseless others at his side
In the implementation of his own suicide?
Or does he, who no longer has the will to live
Take some perverse pleasure in the pain that he gives
And in seeing mirrored that same helplessness he feels
Over some gnawing grievance imagined or real
Find some sense of personal satisfaction
In that final act of self-attraction?
We may never know!

TWO MOTHERS

I had two mothers.
Each cared for me in her own way.
One was distant, biological.
The other near, strict, logical.
I had two mothers.
Now I have none.

UNKIND

I never thought life could be so unkind
To one I love while still in his prime,
Constantly being bombarded with so much affliction
Coming at him cruelly without prediction.
Always he's exemplified kindness in his life
To which I can attest, being his wife.

So why do storm clouds o'er him keep rolling?
He whose virtues we should be extolling.
None of this does he deserve
For others he's always had kindness in reserve.
So let it be over, let it be through
He's the best; he's passed the test with nothing to prove.

UNTITLED

I watched the tears
As she recalled
The anguish of it all
Against personal loss a fight she waged
But in the end death was unphased
She could not change the inevitable
Even tho' strong and seemingly invincible
Along that path she struggled virtually alone
The absence of others hard to condone
In family oft the least revered steps up—while others
deny
And we are left to wonder why.

UNWISE DECISION

Somebody's baby.
There is no maybe.
Horrific accident happened.
Parental pain runs rampant.
All dead and mangled
In steely wreckage tangled.
Unwise decision in an instant made
Finds five young people in coffin laid.

VIOLENCE

Violence unimaginable.
Hands bound behind
No hope for the victim to find.
Weapon pressed to the back of the head
With its resound, anger fed.
And to compound the message making it more dire
The murdered body set afire.
A young man's life ended
Over a mistake made, perpetrators offended.
Heard so often another mother's crying voice
Over a lost son's unwise choice.

WE'RE DONE

I ain't yo' baby no more.
So be prepared for what I got in store.
For I know you cheated big time on me.
I'm walkin' away; it's just my back you'll see.
'cause my love is sour like milk sittin' in the sun.
And you and me, we're over, we're done.

WHAT DID SHE THINK?

At age six what did she think
When to her school with a gun the man came?
Did she call out our name?
Mama, Daddy.

What did she think
When the man fired the gun?
Some new kind of fun?
But there was blood.
Mama, Daddy.

What did she think about the man?
Was she confused
Or in stark terror?
Thinking all this must be in error.
Mama, Daddy.

What did she think?
A dark haired man was there with a gun.
Down her best friend fell
She just must not be well.
Mama, Daddy.

What did she think
When she saw the man's eyes?
Was her teacher nearby?
Did she tearfully watch her die?
Mama, Daddy.

What did she think
When the man raised the big gun?
When she saw it, did she try to run?
Mama, Daddy.

What happened, what did she think?
She could not easily breathe.
Don't hurt me mister please.
Mama, Daddy.

What did she think
As she lay there?
Did she call out our name
We never came.
Mama, Daddy.

What do we think
That December day when the man came?
Once somebody's baby, somebody's son
He decided to kill our child, not the gun.
Mama, Daddy.

WHEN I AM GONE

When I am gone
You'll dream of me.
Be sure.
When I am gone
You'll think of me
Be clear.
When I am not here
You'll be sorry.
When I am gone
Your heart will long for me.
When I am gone.

WHY DON'T YOU COME?

I don't know if I can be alone.
Why don't you come? Why don't you phone?
My life I live just for you.
Without you, consequences quite a few.
Lost I'll be in my own world,
Doors closed, no flags unfurled.
My heart is broken, you've closed me out.
I'm here, can't you hear me shout?
Oh, please, don't leave me here alone.
Why don't you come? Why don't you phone?

Love

Plain and Simple

A CHILD'S LAUGHTER

Open and gleeful is a small child's joyous laughter,
A sound to preserve in the heart ever after.
With a spirited spontaneity it resounds on the ear,
Unencumbered by any legitimate care or fear.
It lightens a heavily burdened soul,
And brightens a day that may have taken its toll.

ALL ABOARD

Your train came 'round the bend
When I thought true love was at an end.
You brought a freight car full of joy
Right off you were my best boy
You made my sorry heart sing
With the bouquets of laughter you did bring.
So I took my chances and hopped on board
With far more happiness than I could afford.

Yeah, with you and love 'twas all aboard.

ANNIVERSARY

For fifty years we've walked the path.
We've loved and cried and more often laughed.
Our journey has taken many a turn,
Yet through it all we've had time to learn
That love and trust are what we do best,
And the two of us are truly blessed.

BREATHE

You're not here
But I feel you breathe.
'twas from this lovin' bed you said you had to leave.
I could not believe those sharp words I heard
How could this be, it was way too absurd.
So early I learned that the things you love best
O'er time oft do not stand up to the test
But tonight tho' you're not here lying next to me
I still feel you breathe.

FALLING IN LOVE?

Falling in love is like a psychosis
Or a drug or peculiar osmosis.
And during this hiatus from reality
The world shimmers with a surfeit of creativity.
Poetic senses are honed
Love babble texted and phoned.
And no one exists but just you two
And then it's over...

GREAT LOVE

I stopped time from touching you.
I loved you and you were always the same for me.
And I believe that is the way
A truly great love ought to be.

HOW
(TO SUZANNE)

How right it felt when I held you in my arms.
How quickly I succumbed to the joy of an infant's charms.
How amazed I was that to me you were to belong.
How insecure I felt, worried I might do you wrong.
How you made me aware of all the wonder love brings.
How you made me laugh over so many things.
How your achievements, large and small,
filled my being with pride.
How I felt your pain when you stumbled and unhappy,
inside or aloud you cried.
How I wanted to absorb any hurt that came your way.
How weak I felt when I knew I could not do it,
each and every day.
How beautiful you were as I watched you grow.
How I loved helping you find answers
to all you wished to know.
How I rejoiced when your longed-for goal was reached.
How I knew with this tool you could survive,
even when besieged.
How proud I am when I observe your generous,
caring heart.

How your compassion for all things, sets you far apart.
How delightful are the children you call your own.
How much of you I see in them,
as they have thrived and grown.
How I hope you have heard my lessons, though not
always immediately understood.
How fervently I pray that I have given you
the very best that I could.
And though I may not be here for you to see,
My enduring love will be your legacy.

LOVE SONGS

How many love songs can there be?
I think I've heard at least one hundred thirty-three.
But when it comes to love there can be no surplus.
Words to express that feeling, a definite must.
The music makes love all the more delightful,
But I am not so certain, any more insightful.

LOVE

When I first saw you, I loved you.
I know that sounds clichéd.
But many years have come and gone
And my instincts have not been betrayed.

When I first saw you, I loved you.
I knew you were to be in my life.
You emanated love and kindness,
Which was what I needed, not strife.

When I first saw you, I loved you.
You have been my faithful friend.
We have waltzed through life together
Facing jointly all that we've had to contend.

When I first saw you, I loved you.
This has always been the case.
These fifty years you've been the only one
To hold my heart in place.

MARRIAGE ANNIVERSARY 58

Reminiscing, I looked at the wedding pictures
Not without a tear in my eye
How did so many years fly by
How thin and wide-eyed we were that day
How different the times, what can I say?

So hard to accept this romance coming to an end
How can there be so little time left to spend
Here together in concert, as we've always been
Sharing life's ups and downs without end
Loving each other from that youthful start
Never yearning to be long apart

Few cross words o'er the years
Just severe illness striking up fears
Knowing today our connection is ever strong
In honoring that pledge to each other to belong
And on this anniversary I can say without doubt
Love and respect is what it's all about.

MY GALLANT MAN

What a lovely gallant man was he,
Plain it was for all to see.
And when first we kissed under the oaken tree,
I knew forever he was mine to be.
So when he asked me to be his wife,
"Yes", I said, and shared his life.
What a lovely gallant man was he.
How amazed I was that he wanted me!

THAT'S WHY I STAYED
(FOR JACK)

Young I was, unsure of who or what I wanted to be.
I had places to go and things to see.
Completely ambivalent was I about my life
With no intention then of being a wife.
You were young and handsome, that's for sure
Instinctively I knew your love would endure.

A few other beaus came my way
But I was not by them at all swayed
'cause there you were with that twinkle in your eye
'twas there for me alone to spy
And with it and your sweet grin displayed
You made me laugh that's why I stayed.

There were other things that could be weighed
But always with you the music played.
So here we are six decades together
And there have been storms that we have weathered
But that choice was right so long ago made
A love destined to flourish, ne'er to fade
For you still make me laugh, that's why I've stayed.

VALENTINE'S DAY
(LOVE IS IN THE AIR)

On this day they say love is in the air
Singing to me and my love so fair.
Hearing sweet violin strings reminds me so
Of the love in his eyes that I alone know.
Vividly I recall the special memories we cherish
Ours forever 'til we should perish
From the moment we both met
Our hearts became an immediate duet.
Always he'll be my valentine
My heart's home for all time.

VIXEN

She's a pretty little vixen
And she be fixin' to steal your heart
To tear your addled brain apart.
You won't know who you are.
She'll be leadin' you on, takin' you afar.
Then watch out with you she'll be done
And that lil' vixen'll be the one who won.

WISHING

I'd forgotten that your words could be so sweet.
It was so long ago when first we did meet.
But here you are in my life once again
And me wondering whether lover or friend.
Wishing both.

YOU SAW ME

You saw me when I was shy,
I could not soar, could not fly.
A fledgling in the arena of emotion,
Of love, I had no inkling, no notion.
You saw strength in me when I saw none
With tenderness my fragile heart you won.
In me your faith was formidable.
Ah you, you saw me when I was invisible.

Memories

Plain and Simple

ALL THAT JAZZ

My baby cried when she heard all that jazz.
It brought out old emotions she once had.
Memories of those Chicago days
Gone so long ago, some now in a haze.

Boot-legged hooch hidden behind a door
And the music was there like never before.
Musicians playing 'til dawn did break
Outdoing each other as though lives at stake.

Patrons infused by the sound and the drink
To go home early was not in their think.
And my baby was there to see it all
When she was young, long, lean and tall.

BACK IN TIME

I want to go back in time,
When there were still mountains to climb
And life was flower fresh and new,
Replete with lovers gallant, quite a few.
The magic was everywhere
And I was not afraid to dare—
Whatever I chose!

BILLIE HOLIDAY

When Lady Day sang the Blues
If you weren't listenin', you must 'a been fools.
With that reedy instrument that was her voice
She sang the songs her way, her choice.
Her voice had about it little range
Effective and poignant all the same
Hitting meaningfully each word the lyricist wrote
Emotion exuding with every note.
Her renditions were done with intensity and pain
She pulled you in so you felt the same.
To pay her way she played dives and pubs
Thrilled audiences at the Apollo and the best of clubs.
Sadly, though, her own life was not the best
'Twas cut short by drugs, drink and all the rest.
Her recordings still haunt whenever played
Thus gratefully for us her memory has stayed.
God Bless The Child!

CHARLTON HESTON

Another star has fallen from the cinematic sky.
A man of Midwestern values who reached the apex of his
ambition
Playing notable characters, heroes in their given
condition.
Now life's drama for him is done
In spite of awards and accolades won.
Will another luminary rise to take his place?
I doubt so. He was a man of grace.

CLASH OF WILLS

When I was young, lady locket, she would say,
You must do chores before you play.
That protestant ethic was hers, no doubt,
But not being mine, it made me want to cry out
To defy, to scream and show all my insolence.
But she, stronger willed overcame my resistance,
With stubborn, all powerful unyielding persistence.

DO YOU REMEMBER?

Do you remember
That fourteenth of December
When my child died?
No place could she find to hide.
That fiend killed her and others
And the world stopped for fathers, for mothers.

Our children were not the enemy
To fight back they had no ability.
What evil lurked in that man's soul
What personal disaster made him less than whole?
Do you remember
That fourteenth of December?
I do.

FINGERPRINTS

You left your fingerprints on my heart
And even though long ago we did part
I remember still that you were the one
Who electrified my soul, danced in dreams that I spun.

FOR CORKIE

Oh, how little feet did scurry
When thunder released all its fury.
And where did doggie quickly tuck her head?
You know, I bet, 'twas under the bed.

GRANDMOTHERS

Faint recollections of being rocked and cuddled,
Why does this now seem all so muddled?
I knew she was unhappy with her lot,
I could sense this even when still a tot.
Her life would have been better without me to raise.
She was old, tired, not needing this phase.
Saddled with a child, even a good one like me,
This was not the way she pictured her future to be.
Looking back, I do not know how she was able to endure.
Could I now, as a grandmother, do the same? I am not

sure.

GRANDMOTHER'S CHILD

I am a grandmother's child,
Never any room to run, run wild.
Rigor the key in my upbringing,
Work, regimentation the code of living.
Discipline delivered with deliberate hand,
Emphatically enforcing a verbal reprimand.
Always looking in that eye of flint
For a modicum of love, just a hint.
T'was seldom there for me to see,
No matter how much I wanted it to be.

GRASSHOPPERS

As I watched,
The grasshoppers flew up again,
Disappearing like little memories,
Wafted away by age and care,
Never more to have relevance.

JUST REMEMBER

I love you but right now I don't like you much.
Perhaps I'm just old and out of touch
But I take exception to your choices and behavior
And I no longer can be your forever savior.

Even though I am a member of the family
The majority of time you can barely see me
Except when it's something monetary I can provide
Then you soften me up and by my side you glide.

But I think that's over, you can stay in touch.
Just remember—I love you but right now I don't like you
much.

LAKESIDE WEEKEND

A lakeside weekend with small children there,
Laughter, happy screams filling the air.
Little bodies browning in summer sun's radiant glow,
So many water skills beginning to show.
Tutored by parents with fond recollection
Of their childhood by the lake, recalled with affection.

LOOKING BACK

Looking back did I behave all that badly?
I still question myself ever so sadly.
Each day there was another blow,
To small legs or buttocks and tears would flow.
I have to believe I was just a reminder,
Of lost dreams—gentler, kinder,
And of a tarnished life, one less than perfection
Represented by me and my reflection.
Ah, but o'er the years I have traveled higher ground
And have reveled happily in the love that I've found.

MANY TEARS

So many tears in those early years,
Little from happiness, most from fears.
Tip toeing silently, not to be seen,
Dodging those blows, cruel and mean,
Knowing now, no blame was mine,
Uncertainty healed with the passage of time.

MR. SNOWMAN

The sun came out today,
And melted Mr. Snowman away.
What fun we had constructing him!
The earmuffs he wore were just a whim.
He was ever so stately, ever so tall,
Each part of his body a perfect ball.
But temperature warming was his fate.
We could not save him, it was too late.
Now we await another snowy day
To build his brother. Maybe he'll stay!

PATRICK SWAYZE

He danced like no other
With a strength and vitality that made female hearts
flutter.
He held us all "like Baby" in his arms
And displayed the best of masculine charms.
In his prime only to be cut down
By insidious disease that from this king stole his crown.
But on film where he glowed with magic and finesse,
Forever we will view his agility and prowess
And remember we will what 'twas like to be young.
Buoyed by his spirit now gone and far flung.

PIANO MAN

The piano man banged away
Just for me, I was sure that day.
I heard the vibrance of the music once again.
It loosened my mind, made me spin.
I was transported to a different sphere
With the clamor of those notes, oh so clear.
I remembered those sounds, what they meant to me.
They buoyed me up, they set me free.
I opened up and sang along
Knowing it was exactly where I belong.

RECOLLECTIONS

With this morn's meandering of the mind
Will, I wonder, again ever find
Somewhere in labyrinth's depth
The things I knew but now forget.
For I have lived so many score
I've cast aside experiences that went on before
And filled my mind with current affairs
Concerned myself with others' cares.
But today, thinking back, struggling to retrieve
Those faint recollections of youth are best,
I believe.

THE ICE CREAM TREE

My father's eyes danced with glee,
When he told me of the ice cream tree,
Whose branches all up and down
With giant cones would abound.
Trees planted from his special seeds
And carefully guarded, if you please,
To colorfully grow so stately and tall
With tasty flavors for one and all.
Now I am grown with a child of my own,
But the story still floats through my mind,
From a tall-<u>taled</u> man with a humorous bent,
So loving and enduringly kind.

THE SLED

My sled was new,
With runners two.
Poised on the precipice of a great big hill,
I knew what was to come would be a thrill.
A running start, a belly flop,
Going on forever, not to stop.
Racing at full out speed downhill,
Power in hand to turn at will.
Wind blowing against frosted cheek,
Traveling o'er moguls and a frozen creek.
How strong and daring it made me feel,
Freely sliding with such exuberance and zeal.
I now in age can only observe from afar,
Holding memory's window open ajar.

TOO YOUNG

You're so young, you can't possibly understand
What it was like dancing to a 40's or 50's band.
To have a handsome young man take you by the hand
Hold you firmly at the waist
As to the beat you both kept pace
To stimulating rhythms and soulful blues
Pure magic in my feet in those high-heeled shoes.
And those shimmering gowns that I wore
Sometimes short and oft to the floor
Were part of a wondrous growing up time
Anything was possible for I was in my prime
And I could be whatever I wanted
For then I was brave and truly undaunted.
Thinking back on all those dances attended
As through those school days I dutifully wended
For me those times meant freedom, a hint of romance in
the air
Ah, but you, so young—enough of this discourse—you
probably don't care.

TRAPEZE

In childhood I swung knees crooked o'er the bar.
From upside down seeing near and far.
As breezily the trapeze whipped to and fro,
The blood made my ears and brow blush so.
What freedom and prowess I felt back then.
Will that sensation be mine ever again?

TSUNAMI, ONE YEAR LATER

For me, the televised image of a grieving mother
Burned in my mind like no other.
She had not visited this spot for a year,
But today she came, not without fear
To this place with all its reminders
Of a loss so horrific there to bind her.
For here her child had been abruptly washed away
At her school on just an ordinary day
By a giant tsunami of epic proportions
Twisting buildings and people in lethal contortions.
Standing there, this mother wondered with eyes filled
with tears
About her daughter who was just barely twelve years—
Was she warm on that day?
Did she have her coat when she and others were swept
away?
This poor mother from a prosperous island nation
Never mind, her ethnicity nor her station
For I, as a mother, felt her deep pain
Feeling her grief so difficult to disclaim,
--and my eyes filled with tears.

Patriotism

Plain and Simple

1945

It was 1945
And I was still alive
I'd come ashore
In that forever war
On a beach they called Omaha
Why that name? Was it just a faux pas?
'cause Nebraska it sure didn't seem
It was damn well a bloody battle scene
As the landing craft brought us in o'er the sea
I saw buddies drop all around me
It was rough
But I was tough
And as we fought our way through France
I never questioned my circumstance
I knew there was a job to be done
T'would not be over until we'd won
I remember the end came in May of '45
I'm old now but still alive
I did survive

FOG OF WAR
(For Pete Mercier)

The fog of war followed him home.
Stuck in his mind like a rhyming poem.
Fragments of the experience rising to the surface,
At unexpected moments without reason or purpose.
Death and tragedy in horrendous flashbacks
Of enemies with bayonets or of armored attacks.
No peaceful nights are his to be.
The dreams repeating as he tries to flee.
The horror that he cannot shake.
Good God—How long will it take?
To be at peace, this soul is at stake!

FORT HOOD SHOOTING

Soldiers shot down in ugly rage
An unfounded, unconscionable, deplorable rampage.
Men and women at peace in daily routine
Butchered, by a supposed comrade, in reality a fiend.
Why, we ask, such an unprovoked, horrific deed?
For those preyed upon we ask justice with due speed.

HALF STAFF

Once again flags fly at half staff
This time for a young man loved for his hearty laugh.
At eighteen, dying way before his time
Delivering an unspeakable sorrow for family and friends
left behind.

I can't help but ask why
So many young Americans have to die?
Never to reach their full potential
Lives sacrificed they say, for our freedoms so essential.

Yet when the struggle is done
And no one has truly won
Will we remember those young lives lost
And pray God, at what cost?

JUSTICE MAYBE

Towers fell
In a reign of terrorized hell.
Lives lost and torn
A nation left to mourn
Those who died
And those who strived
To save the many.

As a country should we be glad?
Will it help us feel less sad?
To know this evil perpetrator is dead
That retribution came with a shot to the head?

His ideology still does exist
Others will arise and they will persist
To challenge, to cause us fear
For the freedoms we all hold so dear.

MARINE POSTER CHILD

Young and green.
A boy, just nineteen.
Yet, a Marine.
Trained by the corps.
Equipped for war.
Carrying a gun,
Weighing a ton.
Enveloped in protective gear.
Yet, how does all that keep him from fear?
Will he be steady?
Is he ready?
For all the carnage he will see!

MY DADDY

My Daddy's a Marine.
He travels far, many places he has seen.
But we are happiest and full of joy
When he doesn't do that thing he calls "deploy".

My Daddy's a Marine.
Something called a Lieutenant, it seems.
When home he tells funny stories of when he was a boy.
He gets silly and plays with me and my brother Roy.
I hope he doesn't have to do that thing called "deploy".

My Daddy's a Marine.
He laughs and says he's lean and mean.
But he sighs and tells us he has to leave again
To some place called Afghanistan.
To help some people in trouble there
But I don't think to leave us is ever fair.

My Daddy's a Marine.
When he goes away he reminds us that Mom is queen.
And that we must listen and obey
Because that, of course, is the military way.
But I never want him to go, just stay.

My Daddy's a Marine.
Not to worry he jokes, he's a fighting machine.
But when he gave me my little princess kiss
There was a tear in his eye, I could not miss.
And he held us all so very tight
In a gigantic hug with all his might.

My Daddy's a Marine.
Wounded. What does that mean?
Says Mom, he's not coming home, my dear
But is in a hospital very near
And we will go to see him quite soon,
Perhaps tomorrow, right about noon.

My Daddy's a Marine, my Mom his wife.
Her's, too, is a military life.
To us children she says, "be prepared".
"Seeing Daddy, try not to be scared"
For he has been hurt by an I.E.D.
Something he could not hear nor could he see.

My Daddy's a Marine.
What I wonder is an I.E.D.?
Just then I see my Daddy way so brave
And he has no arms, to us he cannot wave.
But I run to him to get my kiss and my hug.
'cause my Daddy's home and he's a Marine.

SECOND TOUR OF DUTY

The drum is banging.
Once again my country's calling.
How many more fear filled days must I spend
In defense of those, not of my kin?
While in my home crying children wait,
Ever mindful I, worrying about their fate.
How and when will I return,
Is a constant pounding, a true concern.
But go I must, duty is my master,
Praying the while that I do not meet disaster.

SOLDIER'S LETTER

Two weeks ago the letter came,
And I tenderly placed it in a drawer by my bed,
'cause the message on the wrinkled envelope said,
"Do not read this unless I am dead."
Tonight I shall read it.

SON

Hey son...
I didn't get to say hello, nor goodbye.
It wasn't that I did not care, did not try.
I could not be there the day you were born,
For I was deployed in a country war torn.

By now you know my holding, kissing you was not to be,
As my life and others was taken by an I.E.D.
But mom told me that you were a beautiful baby boy,
And wow, was I puffed up, full of joy!

When you're older she'll tell you all about me
How much I loved her and you ever so completely.
And when people ask about your Dad
Say—he was a proud Marine, one of the best the corps
had.

Semper Fi !

SORROW

Another grieving mother,
Losing a son to a war like no other.
The little boy with the crooked smile,
Whose "love ya, Mom" could instantly beguile.
Who or what will now fill her heart?
That unbreakable bond that was there at the start.
Will she ever completely recover?
As a nation her sorrow is ours to discover.

TAPS

He came home to us last night
From that war, that far off fight.
He left, a Marine, early in the fall
Fresh faced, young and tall.
In Spring they brought his body home
Thankfully, he was not alone.
An honor guard accompanied him
With stuttered step, uniformed and trim.
Seeing him encased in coffin steel
Mournfully nothing was left to feel.
At grave site prayers so softly spoken
Sincere, a sorrow filled, loving token.
And from a grateful nation, a tri-fold flag extended
Even though our hearts were not yet mended.
Rifles were fired in final salute
For our little boy so brave, so resolute.
And in this resting place he was not alone
For there were other comrades who had come home.
Then an unearthly quiet did reign
Complete with finality and oh, such pain.
God help us!
In this stillness the hymn played far too oft of late
For our child and those who had met a similar fate.

We heard Taps. T'was ended
God bless! Amen.

THE DOOR

It was over.
We waited but he did not come home.
We waited but he did not phone.
We waited days, a week
To hear his voice, to hear him speak.

Then came a knock at our door.
It must be him, ah, to wait no more.
But t'was a solemn faced uniformed Marine,
Not our boy, yet hardly much older did he seem.

With hat under arm, he stood poker straight
And sadly reported we no longer need wait.
Alive, our only child would not return from war.
Never again would he walk through that door.

THEY DIED

They died for you, they died for me.
One could say that's the way it's supposed to be.
They are soldiers after all.
But in that logic I say—there's flaw.

For they are daughters, they are sons.
They are all about you, the very ones
Who watched your children, mowed your lawns
And in a thankless foreign war are simply pawns.

For what purpose, what change can they affect?
To me in this type of government think—there is defect.
Call me isolationist, if you wish
But speak to that mother whose child she no longer can
kiss.

TOUR OF DUTY

Obliged am I to be,
Far from loved ones, you see.
Fighting in a foreign land
Tho' not exactly what I'd planned.
For I am bound to sorely miss,
A Daddy's very first little princess kiss.
'cause so tiny was she when I deployed,
Who knows what of her "first things" I could've enjoyed.
She won't know me when home I come,
A stranger I'll be and she—year one.

WORLD WAR II LETTERS

I didn't need anyone else but him, you see
'cause my heart was where it was supposed to be.
But he loved his country as well as me
And he went with others across the sea.
For our country's democracy he was fighting
But he loved and missed me he said in the letters he was
writing.

To him I was sending the same message too
Over the days, months and years our correspondence grew.
Those notes so important were our only connection.
The words inscribed carried mutual love and affection.
All his letters I placed in an empty shoe box
But suddenly without notice his letters stopped.

I continued writing all the while
Worrying would I ever again see that dimpled smile...
Then from the Army I heard captured he had been
And would not be coming home 'til the war was at end.

So I wrote him each day in great detail
Putting the letters in the shoebox, not in the mail.
Unexpectedly a telegram arrived on a bright Sunday morn
And I was left weeping, my heart irreparably torn.
For me all that was left was in the shoebox contained
Those expressions of love and longing were all that
remained.

Thoughts

Plain and Simple

A FEW BIRTHDAYS

I am a woman of a few birthdays.
No patience have I for any questioning of my ways.
I've earned the right to speak my piece.
It exhalts my spirit, gives me release.
So if, perchance, you bravely think to contradict,
Be sure of yourself and the battle you have picked!

BLUE

My color is blue
Any shade or hue.
My eyes it enhances
Lets my psyche take chances.
Good Karma is with me, happy thoughts spew
When I'm attired in my best blue.

BIG BLACK CAR

I got the blues,
'cause today I heard the news.
That you are comin' back my way,
They says you' gonna be wantin' to stay.
Who do you think you are?
You in your big black car.
Who you tryin' to shine up?
Someone younger, some new little pup?
I was your woman, gave you my best.
You said you loved me, mo' than the rest.
But all the same, you walked out on me
Said the big old world you had to see.
You in your big black car.
Guess you travel'd way a far.
Now you be comin' back right here,
But not near me or for your life you'll fear.
You in your big black car!

BLEEDING

Broad smile facing the day.
Inside knives cutting away.
Outward pleasant.
Inside bleeding.

CAR WASH

Once again through the car wash I have gone.
Moved along like a remote controlled pawn.
Slowly traveling at a measured pace,
Claustrophobic sensations having to face.
Sadistic, noisy flapping belts of leather
Like flaying whips from the land of nether.
Rotating brushes aimed at chewing me up,
Sudsy splatters falling from high up above.
Air in bursts makes the passage complete,
Bright light ahead signals the end of the beat.
The car reflects its pristine condition.
And me? I've survived. I am back from perdition.

CELL TOWERS

Cell towers visible on the horizon
Where once a tall maple, pine stood.
Steely indicators of a different world
Less peaceful, less understood.
If their purpose be communication,
Do they truly fulfill expectation?
For these replacements of nature's harmony
Do not speak eloquently to me.

COMPUTER

My computer is a dragon
Ingesting my information
Swallowing my thoughts
Deciding what tastes good
Spitting out the rest with fiery delivery.

CONCRETE

Concrete, how thick? How many feet?
Able to support tall buildings and bridges replete.
Ribbons rolled out in highways,
Crossing country and byways.
Spanning water and rivulet.
America is concrete!

COOKING

Lately my cooking has become suspect.
The reason for this I can't seem to detect.
I have difficulty thinking of things to prepare.
Truth be told, I really just don't care.
So, my dear, don't belly up to my table
For you'll find that I'm no longer capable.
The chicken will undoubtedly be tough and dry
Probably you can't chew it, should you try.

This isn't the way things used to be
Always I felt a well-made meal my responsibility.
But years have come and years have gone
And menus planned have repeatedly gone wrong.
So I think I'll hang up my poofy chef's hat
And you know,—I'm not worrying at all about that.

CORDUROY PANTS

My corduroys are making music.
I bet you think that sounds confusing.
But when I walk ever so rapidly,
With each step my pants sing quite happily.

DANDELION DREAMS

With clouded eyes she saw patches of dandelions, like she,
past their prime.
They reminded her of days gone by, an earlier place in time.
Nostalgically she reached down and picked a few,
So representative they were of the childhood days she once
knew.
Remembering, she blew on the silver gray dandelion
whiskers,
Making a wish and crossing her fingers.
She watched them ethereally ascend into the blue,
Carrying long forgotten dreams with them, as they flew.

DEFINITION

Do not define me by your standards.
You are not my measuring stick.
Do not define me by your prejudices.
They are not necessarily mine.
Do not define me by what you think you know of me.
I am not your mirror image.
I am my own person with my own values.
I know my worth and my own mind.

DEMONS

I awoke in very early morn
From sleep I was irreparably torn
By subconscious demons in my brain
Who in slumber stealthily came
To disrupt my nightly rest,
Even tho' I tried my concerted best
To shut them out!

DETROIT CITY

The repo man has come to the city
Good God, who'd have thought, what a pity!
A once grand metropolis in such dire straits
On edge expecting the edict that awaits
How could have such a thing occurred
To the Motor City mecca long preferred
By those who wanted to earn a decent wage
In a time when that was difficult at any age
But through the years there was misplaced trust
And the money grubbing elected accelerated
the bust
Of the once great city, the Arsenal of Democracy
With all their lies and unbridled hypocrisy
And so dear citizens, I see little hope
Just suck it up, hunker down and cope

DRAMA

So much intense drama in my life.
Actors playing roles consumed by strife.
Good God, let these tragic scenes come to an end,
Let me say it's over; let me recite good night, amen.
Quickly ring down that heavy dust laden curtain
So this play will be over, the finale for certain.

ENOUGH

I've had enough.
I need to be tough.
What more can I say—
Like Clint, "come on make my day!"
'cause I'm lookin' straight at you
And what you're doin' is ugly, it is true
So I'm gonna deal with it and with you
Hey, mister, you're just bad clear through.

EVIL

I cannot believe the evil I hear.
Crimes against those most vulnerable are the worst,
it's clear.
Killings, beatings and burnings of defenseless little ones,
Abuse of adoptees, daughters and sons.
How can we begin to justify this shame in our society?
What these perpetrators need is an eye for an eye!

FALLING LEAVES

What if falling leaves were like wishes
That we could gather up
And in their abundance
And by some magical incantation
Make someone's life better?

FLAWED

We are all flawed.
We trade on ambivalence.
Our conscience fluctuates between right and wrong.
Decision comes at a cost.
Will our souls be lost?

GIVING UP THE STRUGGLE

I'm thinking of giving up the fight.
I have struggled with main and might
To keep our lives as once they were
But illness is in every corner causing a stir
So now I must acknowledge it's time to bend
For against devils and demons 'tis difficult to defend.
And when it's time, I'll lay down the sword
Unwilling to continue against the multiplying hoard.
And would that God be by my side
For in him my resolute faith does abide
And then I'll look forward to peace.

GOD BUT…

You have your god but…
Do I have mine?
Is there something by way of a sign
That I should recognize?
Something large, of a size,
That will show me the way,
Put faith in play?
I look about me all the while.
For a reason to believe.

GUN

In the future if we should go to the mall
Will there be signage mounted on a wall
Stating openly that no guns are permitted
And please no explosive devices exhibited.
I state this, of course, tongue in cheek
As another hooded gunman killed patrons this week.
But for us as citizens the concern is not a phase
As we attend sports events or simply window gaze
Unsettled, we have to wonder if there is a gun nearby
And this morn did we rise, dress, go out, just to die?

HARSH CLIME

'Tis a winter of harsh clime
Difficult to rise spritely sans visible sunshine
Struggle ensues just to get out my door
Chilled as I am to my very core
By blustery winds that batter my body
Even tho' primed by caffeine, my particular hot toddy.
But trudge on I must through snow and ice
'cause I've overslept, my frequent vice
And I'll be challenged by my vociferous boss
Threatening me with the infamous job loss
So smile sweetly I will and with sugar say
"You really look very nice today!"

HIGHWAYS

Highways unfolding
With miles of vehicles
Each full of stories
Of sadness or glories,
Contained for a time
Within the confine
Of their transport.

HOLIDAY

I need a holiday from trouble filled thinking
Where no gritty TV images are constantly blinking.
A time to wipe all cares from mind
A chance to meditate, an inner peace to find
To fill my soul with simple pleasures
To reflect on life's bounties, its multiple treasures
To renew my spirit, to reflect on love
To count all blessings showered from above.

HOT DAYS

In Michigan, how we long for hot summer days,
But this heat and humidity are making me crazed.
The sweat is dripping from my nose,
Even after misting my face with the hose.
My swollen fingers are sticky and icky,
My double chins are icky and sticky.
The only way to possibly cool down,
Is simply not to move any body part around.
So as fickle as we human beings are,
In winter when we're deicing the car,
We'll yearn once again for a long summer's day,
Memory devoid of the role heat and humidity play.

ICICLES

Glistening in sunlight my eye did perceive,
Icicles spiraling down from the eave.
Soldiers in formation strong and robust,
Acute points like bayonets ready to thrust.
Soon in sun's radiance they will disappear,
Leaving mere ice chunks and puddles I fear.
Who then will be there to guard the gate,
Once our stalwart soldiers have met their fate?

ICE AND SNOW

Ice and snow.
Will it ever go?
I hardly dare think so.
To counteract serious fall prevention
The shovel has become my hand's extension
It gives me exercise so rigorous
While combating winter's blast so vigorous
But it can be over now
I've coped - next year the plow!

IRS

'Tis April and as citizens we should be happy
But the IRS is lurking, saying make it snappy.
'cause they want all the money that they can get
No such thing as a break as you might expect.
For if you don't pay up and do it on time,
There'll be penalties and interest and it won't be at prime.
And equally ugly are those officers of revenue
From them you'll hear threats and nothing good will
spew.
For they know how to scare and intimidate
And if you don't acquiesce, jail could be your fate.
So cough up what's owing old buddy, old mate
And whatever you do, don't dare to be late.

KNITTING

I started knitting.
I thought for relaxation it would be fitting.
I carefully counted each stitch I placed,
Making each one uniform on the needle it encased.
But, alas, my stitches were so tight,
Each knit and purl was a fight.
I shoved and tugged with gnarled hand,
Attempting to create a simple hat band.
With disposition extremely distraught,
Brow sweaty, plainly overwrought,
I thought it best to put those needles away,
Perhaps to attempt relaxation another day.

LIGHTEN UP

Lighten up!
Let it go!
All the veins in your forehead show.
Life's too pleasing
To be releasing
Venom such as yours!

LISTS

Lists upon lists I make
Of things I want to do
Keeping me focused, so I'll follow through.
But for some peculiar reason,
They never seem to work
'cause I forget to read them, that being my quirk!

MICHIGAN NORTH

I sit in solitude on woodland's brink
Letting my mind wander and I think
I hear ghosts eerily whispering in the pines
Speaking of the past, their times
Of how they were attracted to this setting that I see
Where woods and water meet in exquisite harmony.
I hear them clearly and I must confess
I know in just being here, I am truly blessed.

MISTAKES

My brain is on fire.
I am walking a high wire.
How to master
Saving loved ones from disaster.
Too many mistakes have been made.
Too many games have been played.
I think I have used up all my skills.
I know not how to prevent this clash of wills.
Advice given, little taken.

MONEY

I sit like Midas counting my money.
By Jove, I bet you think that's funny
But I always wait for the drop of that shoe
Wondering if I'll have enough to get me through.

MY LIFE'S STAGE

I grab happiness wherever I can,
'cause at my stage of life 'tis oft not the plan.
Days are spent visiting those who administer
Varieties of medications impacting ills, oh, so sinister.
And each morn as I arise,
I try to be vigilant, try to be wise
And look for little things that offer delight—
A child's laughter, a song, a bird in flight,
For each in its way brightens the spirit
And centers me on the import that each can bring with it.
So please, come laugh and smile with me, if you will,
And believe, in life, there are good things still.

MY MUSE

Have I lost my magical muse?
Has this all been a mean-spirited ruse?
My pen is not working,
My duty I'm shirking,
A single line I cannot find,
To unlock the labyrinth of this cluttered mind.

MY POEMS

My poems are like a personal diary.
Traveling with me along life's highway.
Uttering a constant rhyme
In the way I perceive life at any given time.
The feelings and the emotion
The love and the devotion
The poems are like therapy
Some to be shared for all to see
Others not.

NEAR CRAZY

I escaped from near crazy
By writing down everything in rhyme.
The process got me through those fierce dark times.
With pen on paper of each piece
I was able to experience release.
The rhymes expanded and I was saved
As the words took shape on each page displayed.

NIGHT FRIGHT

They're back again.
Nightmares that in my brain careen.
Twisting around some gory, bloody scene.
Murder and mayhem all about.
A victim uttering a voiceless shout.
Freud and Jung would have a field day with me,
These nocturnal images are as bold as on TV.
Vainly I try to wake from this horror so paramount.
What I need is a remote to completely shut them out.

NIGHTMARES

Nightmares come each night
Accompanied by horrific fright
As tho' they had been writ
To fulfill a cinemaker's noir film script.
And I, on awakening with trepidation
Know not if in reality or fiction.

NO KALE

I can't eat that, it's green!
Others of you out there must know what I mean.
'cause for me there is an edible aversion, you see
To colors and textures that such food may be.
So if you think to make healthy my day,
No kale for me is what I will say!

NOVEMBER EXCEPTION

November should be blustery
With autumnal winds cold and gusty.
But today 'tis warmth I feel,
So giddy am I that I veritably reel
In the joy of this Indian summer day's excitement
Postponing still, winter's cruel indictment.

OH SHIT!

Oh shit!
Those words from you just don't fit
My image of a lady so refined,
Of placid demeanor ever so kind.
Yet I agree, when life does not go smoothly,
Oh shit sums it up ever so uncouthly!!!

ONE LEFT

A single valiant flower left
In what once was a resplendent garden
Of brilliant blooms.

In life, like the garden
There is now a single being
The remainder of an intellectual circle.

Left behind by a clan of friends and scholars
All decimated by ills and disease
All gone to ashes.

Still this one stalwart stalk stands
Able yet to pass on wisdom and knowledge
But for how long?

OUTSIDER

Always on the outside, always looking in.
What an enigmatic life this has been.
Has my presence here been noted?
Would anyone for me have voted?
Whom have I touched? Whom have I aided?
Or is my outlook merely jaded?

PANTIES

I wear granny panties because I should
But if I were younger, I know I would
Wear those lovely, lacey undies, oh so skimpy
Victoria secret pretty, I'd not be wimpy
And I would go confidently about my day
Grinning, knowing underneath, I was doing it my way.

POLITICS

'Tis the political season
Candidates babble, oft without reason.
Why should we believe one o'er the other?
The search for any real truth is so difficult to discover.

QUIET

Of late I have been living in quiet.
No techno sounds bombarding me.
A tranquil feeling has come to be.
I hear the singing of birds and can locate them.
The quietness provides serenity.
I am at peace in my mind and in my world.

RAGAMUFFIN

Ragamuffin, what a funny word.
How absurd.
For 'tis not a muffin nor a rag,
But we think, a Dickens child with no name tag
In dirty, ill-fitting clothing quite despicable
With mischief in his eyes, ah, so predictable.
So let's grab him and clean him up
To turn him into a respectable pup.

RANDOM ACT

Can one anticipate extreme killing and its impact
The randomness and cruelty of such a deadly act
By a seemingly frail killer of unlikely countenance
Bearing a weapon almost too big to balance.
We're left wondering about what one can do
When to us, unbeknown, the mind snaps evil!

RED CAR

In my dotage I bought a shiny red car
Hoping it would speedily take me far
Away from my less than satisfying real life
Filled with concern about others in strife.
The car is but symbolic of what I want life to be.
For in my heart it is from trouble I just want to flee.

SAFE WORLD

I created a safe world for myself.
Anything that I imagined could be mine.
In the outside world I could spend time.
Of my other dreary world I showed no sign.

For many years this was the path I walked
Until one day I felt safe and I talked
About those times ever so painful
About treatment ever so shameful.

With revelation the two worlds merged
Sorrows were over, at last purged.
And with the change in times and attitude
I found forgiveness, peace and gratitude.

SCAT

The words fell out of my mouth.
I tol' you, scat, get away from me, go south.
'cause I got it all figured out
And in my mind there ain't no doubt
That you and me just don't belong.
For us there's no lovey-dovey love song.
So be honest, you're a knowin' it too
We're over, we're just through!

SECRET

All lips had to be sealed.
The secret and disappointment could not be revealed.
The shame was in an act forbidden.
The burden was to keep it hidden.
In me the knowledge was always there,
Heavy, pressing almost more than I could bear.
The only escape was to grow up and leave,
Ripping the dishonorable badge from my sleeve,
Vanishing, dissolving into the crowd,
So perhaps in anonymity find a way to be proud.

SLEEP

Sleep is just an illusion.
My mind is in total confusion.
Thoughts dancing persistently through my head
No rest comes in this toss, turn bed.

SLEEPING, DREAMING

Sleeping, dreaming without meaning.
Meaning not to be dreaming, but sleeping
Or simply sleeping and dreaming with meaning.
Still tired!!

SNOW ANGEL

Snow angel, snow angel with white flapping wings,
What a wonderful thing a snowy day brings!
We flop back to the ground arms o'er our head
On soft piles of snow like a great feather bed.
Legs, arms, pushing, pulling, laughter filling our ears
'til wonder of wonders a snow angel appears.

SUMMER'S END

As along life's path I wend
Another summer coming to an end.
It seems it just began for me,
And bam! 'twas over in a flash—one, two, three.

And I'm left wondering where
The days have gone with none to spare.
With all those things left undone
People not seen, stories unspun.

In the harsh winter months that lie ahead,
I know I'll face them with certain dread
All the while planning for beauteous spring
And anticipating what another summer will bring.

SUNSET

Sunset, clouds stretched thinly o'er the horizon.
Birds making final evening flights.
Loons calling plaintively to one another.
No wind driven ripples on the water this eve
To disturb the stillness of the scene.
Calm and quiet all about.
Would that my soul could be absorbed into this picture.

SURPRISE

We expected one.
And out came four.
Relieved we were that there weren't more.
'cause all we have is just one crib.
The same could be said for baby's bib.
Two pair of twins identical
No girls, just boys, what a miracle.

SUZY'S LOAN

I need money, a sizeable loan
For which I've spent hours and hours on the phone.
And visiting financial institutions, those fluorescent banks
Where they smile benignly and accept my thanks.
Say they'll call in due time
While ushering me out with info on prime.
In the interim, I know not where to turn.
My wits are at end, my stomach a'churn.
So I have decided to give the Land of Oz a try,
Hoping against hope to catch the Wizard on fly.
For he gives out courage, hearts and brains.
That's what I've heard, that's what he claims.
So perhaps in the Emerald City he has an extra
money bag,
A big fat heavy one and on it my name tag.

TAXES

Taxes seem to have a life of their own.
An experiment, an unearthly clone.
Growing on all fronts like repugnant weeds.
Planted by municipal, township or federal government
seeds.
Trying to combat them is essentially futile
For if a tax disappears once in a while
Another more heinous fills that crack
And a new vicious variety is ultimately back.
One that springs up and expands
And no amount of complaining or shrill demands
Kills it.

TECHNO CRASH

I have tried to soar into the golden orb of technology
But no matter how hard I try
Technology just keeps passing me by
And even with effort determined, heart felt
The wax on my wings always does melt
And I, like Icarus, crash...

THE CALENDAR

Numbers in squares
Ordering each day's affairs
Ticking off with persistence
Those all-important appointments that define our
existence.
With the monthly turn of the page,
We could perhaps our whole life rearrange,
Just by not noting anything next to the number,
Our lives we could joyfully unencumber.

THE CLOSET

When you're a child a closet is a scary place.
There may be a man within hiding his boogey face.
When you're a teen, it contains all your possessions,
The latest and the ultimate of youth's pimply obsessions.
Then in comes adulthood with its many sizes,
What will look the best on me? One vainly surmises.
As we age, the closet stores long forgotten treasures,
Which in their day were a source of numerous delightful
pleasures.
Through life's passage the closet tells the moving tale
Of all life's currents in reflected detail.

THE DRESSING ROOM

Trying on dresses is exasperating work,
One that women oft defer, frequently shirk.
Too much or too little from which to choose,
Best tackle the job with a shot full of booze.
But for those wonderful women along in years,
The dressing room can confuse, 'til memory clears.
Such a woman as this with her eyes a glaze,
And an absent mind deep in a haze,
Poignantly raised this question aloft,
Can you tell me—am I putting this on or taking it off?

THE FLOWER

Ah, 'tis but a simple flower
But its smile has such miraculous power
To brighten a less than lovely life
Filled with pain, filled with strife.
And confined within its soft, silken fold
Its perfume releases therapy untold
To ease the tension of the mind
And bring solace of a gentle kind.

THE HERON

In misty morn the heron takes his stalwart stance
Waiting for the sun to dance
On rippled waters of gray and blue.
And with feathered wings warmed clear through,
He lifts in flight for a distant shore,
A majestic sight as I watch him soar.

THE KITE

What if I were a magnificent kite,
And with a puff of wind, I took flight?
Guided by a long and elegant tail,
Flowing out behind like a bride's white veil.
I would soar up into a fluffy cloud,
Dip and bob in the cottony mound.
Flying o'er mountains with snowcapped noses,
To distant lands that I have chosen.
When at last I deemed it time to return,
I would land with finesse on grass or fern.
What an endless yarn I would spin,
Telling of my adventures and where I had been.

THE LOOKING GLASS

My friend had surgery on her eyes,
And much to her chagrin and her surprise,
When in the looking glass she chanced to peer,
She was startled and withdrew in fear.
For she saw wrinkles she didn't know she had,
And, oh my goodness, they were bad.
So now another decision to be made,
Not being able to accept this beauty fade.
What cosmetic doc should she pick?
To fix her up and mighty quick!

THINKING CAP

I put on my thinking cap.
Nothing happened in a snap.
No profound idea like Einstein's came my way
No humanitarian project came into play,
So perhaps my cap is faulty or too tight on my head,
'cause nothing extraordinary from my feeble mind sped.

TIP OF MY TONGUE

It was on the tip of my tongue to say
But then my brain meandered and the thought went away
But wait around
And I'll rebound
For I'm excited for you to hear
Oh yes, you with your very own ear
That thought of mine that abruptly went away
Whatever it was that my tongue and its tip had to say.

TO DANCE

I loved to dance
Whenever I got the chance
In a whirling skirt or tight fitting pants.
That rock and roll
It just filled my soul.
Whoa!!!

TOAST

If you asked what I like to eat the most,
My response would undoubtedly be wheat toast
With coffee each morn I consume slices three
It starts my day off just as I want it to be.

And should I perchance miss this first meal
Everything in my day unwinds like a reel.
Not a breakfast of champions I'm sure you'd agree
But 'tis the one that works the very best for me.

WORDS

Crazy words and thoughts run through my head
In early morn when I'm abed
They become a gnawing pest
Precluding any peaceful rest
'til I arise and write them down.

TRILLIUM

Splashes of white along the roadside,
Delicate petals by woods edge abide.
Casting off Winter, having survived,
Proclaiming once more, Spring has arrived.

TRUCKS

Trucks high-balling down the road.
What puts the drivers in this vengeful mode?
Time is money is what they say.
So you damn well better get out of their way.

VALIDATION

We all need to be validated.
Perhaps that sounds jaded
But for life to have meaning,
Our feathers need preening.

WALKIN'

Each morning alone I go a'walkin'.
It gives me respite from TV squawkin'.
Cruising at a feverish pace,
Like the devil and I were in a race.
And as I pound those many steps,
I allow my mind to wander,
Planning all my daily tasks
And to memories from back yonder.
So with heart a pumpin' and muscles a jumpin',
I trod this daily beat,
Through weather cold and weather damp
And lots of summer heat.
And what do I expect to gain?
Other than multiple aches and pain?
Just time for reflecting, clearing my mind,
Searching the soul, my essence to find.

WEATHER

Dark clouds, gray.
T'was supposed to be a sunny day.
The weather prophet on TV
Said pleasant it was going to be.
Friends here, a score or more in congregate,
Do we barbeque or do we wait?
As on the beach we sit and stare
Scanning the west for weather fair.

WHAT DID I DO WRONG?

Anger weighed heavily in the air.
Fear was there.
In a room filled with thunder claps of explosive words,
Blame volleying back and forth in electric spurts,
Two small children on a carpeted floor,
Hunched tensely o'er playthings spread out before,
Trying to process all that they heard,
When one of them stated in a whispered word,
Why are you so mad?
What did I do wrong?
My tears flowed!

WHAT

What did you do down there, my dear?
I was a loving wife for many years of my life.
What did you do down there, my dear?
I was a mother, of a daughter like no other.
What did you do down there, my dear?
I was a proud grandma, who wrote poems and sang *tra la*.
What did you do down there, my dear?
I was a teacher of the mercurial teen creature.
What did you do down there, my dear?
I was a friend to so many without end.
What did you do down there, my dear?
I praised God, that's why I am here.

WINTER SKY

A gray mournful morning sky,
Snow weighted evergreen boughs,
Bending, paying homage as I pass by.
A world silent, in a hush,
A winter's picture painted by an inspired brush.
A peaceful scene without chaos.
Would that it always be so for us.

WORDS

Your words embody—youthful, new, unfulfilled passion.
My words embody—past things, old, out of fashion.
Together our words are rife
With the ups and downs, the seesaw of life.
You, just beginning, all heights abound
While I remain entrenched, solidly aground.

YELLOW BUS

'Tis a yellow bus I see
Parked outside near a tree
Waiting for young riders ever patiently
To rush out the doors as the clock strikes three.
Then to putt-putt on its way
With a load of children in its bay.
The route it follows is in reverse
The morning trip was but to rehearse.

Epilogue

Plain and Simple

GONE

"No one is ever gone until they are forgotten."
Do not forget me.
I love you. I am here.

Celia P. Ransom

After almost thirty-nine years as an educator Celia was obliged to retire as she found herself in the position of caretaker for two of her close family members; her mother and her husband. Since they were not in the same city, Celia found herself frequently on the road and often alone in either a motel room or in her family's lakeside cottage in northern Michigan. During this six year period Celia had many hours of "alone time" and spent much of it in reflection on her life and the world around her.

She had written but one poem in her life prior, but suddenly the words and feelings needed to be expressed and the rhymes just would not leave her head.

Celia wrote and wrote about experiences and feelings and the people in her life. In between, she tried different forms of expression for the fun of it; and wrote a multitude of poems specifically for her grandchildren. The writing helped her be at one with her world and was a release while navigating the rough waters of the health care system. Celia believes that for the reader, many of these poems are universal.

Celia is a self-proclaimed small town girl, even though having lived near the big city for over fifty years. She holds two degrees from Michigan State University, and has enjoyed a fruitful teaching career in secondary education and in the area of teacher training.